Parenting in Christ

Lessons from the Parables

CHRISTINA DRONEN

DEDICATION

To my husband who has encouraged me, afforded me the time to write, and traveled with me on this journey to understand how knowing Christ impacts our parenting.

To my children, my teachers, without whom I'd never dream to embark on such an endeavor.

Most of all I am thankful to Christ who has redeemed so many parts of my life, including family relationships. All wisdom in this literature is from him, any failings the fault of the author.

CONTENTS

ACKNOWLEDGMENTS

This work would not have been possible without the wisdom and support of my church, Pacific Crossroads Church in Los Angeles. In particular, my mom's group at Pacific Crossroads Church, who helped refine and review the material. My sincerest appreciation to Marie Kirchner and Cheryl Baker for the encouragement, wisdom, and enthusiasm in reviewing the material.

ACKNOWLEDGMENTS

PREFACE

Parenting, like any good adventure, can be scary, challenging, and fun. But parents aren't meant just to be along for the ride, we are to lead the way. It's a job that requires us to give up time, money, and energy. We teach our children not just with our words, but also with our behaviors and attitudes, how to understand the world that is seen and unseen. We are more than rule makers and caretakers, we are soul shapers.

In the following lessons we will look at parables and examine the treasures of wisdom and knowledge within that can apply to parenting. Jesus told these parables, or stories, to teach us about who we are, who God is, and the way of God. Within these stories are hidden the secrets of the invisible world and truths to help us live well, like Jesus did.

It is important to bear in mind that although we may follow in Jesus' footsteps, this does not make us the savior. Rather it is through our union with Christ that we can grow into the likeness of Christ. We join with Christ in the work of conforming to his character, and then we are able to more effectively teach our children to do the same.

The following lessons are intended to foster further thought and discussion, not to dole out rules and formulas. It works best as a discussion guide, done in community. At the end of each lesson, a challenge is offered as a way to try on the way of Christ. It's recommended that you encourage and check in with each other as you experiment with these challenges.

All parables quoted here are quoted or adapted from the Easy to Read Version of the Bible.

1

The Gardener

Helping the Truth Take Root and Grow

Ice Breaker

Have you ever tried to grow a plant? How did it go?

Lesson

A large part of parenting is teaching. Teaching is like working in a garden. Gardeners don't plant one day and get fruit the next. They plant, protect, water, and wait to see if good fruit comes from their efforts. Things like the weather, weeds, and type of soil affect how healthy the plant becomes. They can't control some things, like the weather, but they can take care of the soil it's planted in. Like gardeners, parents must work and invest in hopes of one day seeing good things from their children.

Jesus, who compared himself to a gardener,[1] shared this parable about teaching.

> A gardener went out to sow seed. While he was scattering the seed, some of it fell by the road. The birds came and ate all that seed. Other seed fell on rocky ground, where there was not enough dirt. It grew very fast there, because the soil was not

---

[1] Matthew 13:37

1

deep. But when the sun rose, it burned the plants. The plants died because they did not have deep roots. Some other seed fell among thorny weeds. The weeds grew and stopped the good plants from growing. But some of the seed fell on good ground. There it grew and made grain. Some plants made 100 times more grain, some 60 times more, and some 30 times more.[2]

The truth is like a seed and people are like the different kinds of soil. Here's what the parable means about the different kinds of people the soil represents and how a teaching, like a seed, grows in each one.

1. The first type of soil is on the road. It has been stepped on so many times that it is hard. The truth can't sink into it. If a child's mind and heart are hard, afraid of being stepped on, any truth he or she hears won't sink in and grow. Left unprotected, it will be stolen away.

2. The second type of soil is the rocky ground. In rocky ground, there is a little bit of soft soil, so the truth starts growing. But the rocks keep the roots from growing strong and deep. The rocks are the parts that won't let the truth in. So when a child goes through hard times, the roots of the truth that started to grow are too weak. The truth is lost.

3. The third type of soil is full of weeds. The weeds are lies and bad ideas. The seed of truth lands there and they all grow together. The bad ideas and lies were there first and their roots are strong. They take over, killing off the good teaching.

4. Finally, there is the good soil. Children enter the world eager to learn.[3] In fact, several studies have recently published concluding

---

[2] Matthew 13:3-8,"gardener" substituted for "farmer" by the author
[3] Luke 18:17

that babies are "little scientists."[4] For the seed of truth to grow and be strong in them, they must be willing to listen to it and welcome it in like soft soil.

As parents, we can help them to stay soft, pull out the weeds of bad thinking, and keep away those who would steal the truth from them. If we take care of the garden of their hearts and minds, it will strengthen them in the truth and increase the chances that good things will come of their lives.

Questions

1. Which type of soil do you think you are?

2. Which type of soil do you think your child is?

3. In the rocky soil, what do the rocks represent?

4. What is the most important truth or "seed" you should grow in your child's mind and heart?

5. Like the gardener who dropped seeds on all different types of soil, why do you think God gives the truth to all the different types of people?

Trying on the way of Jesus

How can you help your child become better "soil" for growing truth?

---

[4] Alison Gopnik, "Scientific Thinking in Young Children: Theoretical Advances, Empirical Research, and Policy Implications", SCIENCE28 SEP 2012 : 1623-1627.

2

The Guest

Acting with Humility

Ice Breaker

Share an embarrassing story.

Lesson

Humble people honor the value of others. They see their own value too, but they don't believe they more important than other people. It's easy to fall into the trap of thinking we are "better" than other people. Researchers have found that we assume the best in ourselves, but the worst in others.[5] We can become prideful and want to have things our way right away. But this is not how we are supposed to act and think. Proud thoughts will only lead to defeat.[6] Humility is better.

Jesus, who was the most humble man[7] who ever lived, shared this story about humility.

---

[5] "Control blindness: Why people can make incorrect inferences about the intentions of others" by Andrew B. S. Willett, Richard S. Marken, Maximilian G. Parker, and Warren Mansell in *Attention, Perception, and Psychophysics*. Published online January 11 2017.
[6] Proverbs 16:18
[7] Philippians 2:5-8

When someone invites you to a wedding, don't sit in the most important seat. They may have invited someone more important than you. And if you are sitting in the most important seat, they will come to you and say, "Give this man your seat!" Then you will have to move down to the last place and be embarrassed.

So when someone invites you, go sit in the seat that is not important. Then they will come to you and say, "Friend, move up here to this better place!" What an honor this will be for you in front of all the other guests. Everyone who makes themselves important will be made humble. But everyone who makes themselves humble will be made important.[8]

It can be tempting to believe that adults are more valuable than children. By worldly standards, they are. Adults have more power, money, strength, and wisdom. But by God's standards, a child is a gift,[9] greatly valued in His kingdom.[10] Each child is uniquely created by God to serve His purposes. The honor for a parent in being granted the responsibility to care for someone precious to God.

Little children are often more humble than adults. They don't worry about image or what others think of them. They will dance freely, roll in mud, and pass gas like no one's there. They will also ask "silly" questions, take chances, and try new things without the fear of being embarrassed. They know that their place is low and that they have much to learn.

Christ-like humility starts with believing God's opinion about you and valuing it more than any other opinion, including your own. It requires believing that the all-knowing Creator of the universe can make better

---

[8] Luke 14:8-11
[9] Psalm 127:3
[10] Matthew 18:1-6, Matthew 19:14, Matthew 21:16

judgments than you can about who is more important. To act like you are the most important, like the wedding guest did, often leads to humiliation.

Your acceptance by God is not based on how great you are, but how great His love is. When you feel secure in how valuable God says you are, you don't need a seat of honor. You can show your honor and respect for others by taking the low position at the table. You have the confidence to treat others like they are more important, and to leave the seat of honor up to God.

Questions

1. How do you define humility?

2. How should adults be more like children? How should we not be like children?

3. What does it look like to be a humble parent?

4. What's the best way to teach a child to be humble?

Trying on the way of Jesus

Join your child in doing something that requires you to be humble.

3
The Worker

Choosing Gratitude

Ice Breaker

What are you most thankful for?

Lesson

Everyone likes thankful and happy children who appreciate everything done for them. But helping a child become like this is not easy. It requires more than just training a child to say "thank you." A child might say thank you all the time, but still have a bad attitude. What he or she really needs is gratitude. Having gratitude means being thankful and valuing the kindness of the giver. For children to have true gratitude, they must be able to see the difference between what's owed, what's earned, and what's a gift. Gratitude is an attitude of the heart and a sign of good character. It is the cure for entitlement, needed for contentment, and leads to generosity.

When children don't have gratitude, they become selfish. All their focus is on what they want. They forget the good gifts that they have. They start to believe that they should have everything they want without having to work for it. They complain and are angry and unhappy.

Jesus, who was very generous[11] and grateful,[12] shared this story.

> There was a man who owned some land. One morning, the man went out very early to hire some people to work in his vineyard. He agreed to pay the workers one silver coin for working that day. Then he sent them into the vineyard to work.
>
> About nine o'clock the man went to the marketplace and saw some people standing around, doing nothing. So he said to them, "If you go and work in my field, I will pay you what your work is worth." So they went to work in the vineyard.
>
> At about twelve, three, and five o'clock he went and hired more people, who had no work, to work in his vineyard. He said he would pay them "whatever is right."
>
> At the end of the day, the owner of the field had all the workers paid starting with the ones who were hired last. Everyone got paid a silver coin, so the workers who were hired first thought they would be paid more than the others. When they got their silver coin, they complained.
>
> The owner said to one of them, "Friend, I am being fair with you. You agreed to work for one silver coin. So take your pay and go. I want to give the man who was hired last the same pay I gave you. Why are you jealous because I am generous?"[13]

A child, like the worker, needs to be taught an attitude of gratitude. Here are some helpful ideas on how to do that from the story.

---

[11] 2 Corinthians 8:9

[12] John 11:41-42

[13] Matthew 20:1-15 (ERV, with some edits for brevity by the author)

1. Set clear expectations. The owner told everyone that he would pay them one silver coin or "what is right." The workers did what was agreed upon and so did the owner. The first workers hired did not do anything more than they agreed to, so they should not have expected more pay.

2. Help your children identify gifts and blessings and to be thankful for the giver. Just to have work and a silver coin was a gift. Every one of the people who were hired that day started out with no work and one less silver coin. No one earned or was owed a job. They received work and pay because of the kindness of the landowner.

3. Be a good example. Show what it means to be grateful. Speak regularly about all that you are thankful for. Don't complain[14] or talk about all that you are owed. It is tempting to parent by complaint, saying things like, "How many times have I told you? … You drive me crazy … I'm sick and tired of … " But this kind of talk is not helpful. It does not teach your child how to do better.

4. Help your children to see those in need without comparing. The order of hiring that day was not decided by level of need or qualification, but happenstance. The field owner pursued and invited all. Instead of being grateful for having been found and proud of their own work,[15] the workers who were hired first compared themselves to those hired last. In doing so, they became angry and entitled.

5. Teach your child that giving requires effort. Have him work for the gifts he gives. The field owner got up early and went from

---

[14] Philippians 2:14
[15] Galatians 6:4

11

place to place throughout the day looking for people to work in his field. He paid them with his own money. No one got a silver coin for doing nothing, not even the field owner.

6. Remind your child that God determines her value, not position, wealth, or any other worldly indicator. Everyone the owner came across was invited. Though their circumstances were different, they were equally valued and paid.

7. Be generous and thoughtful in meeting the needs of others. When you decide to give a gift, do so without condition just as the field owner gave a job to everyone he came across. Give not just what is desired or asked for, but what is most helpful to the recipient. By giving other people work, the field owner met many more needs than if he had just given them money.

Questions

1. What's the difference between saying "thank you" and having gratitude?

2. Do you find yourself complaining in your parenting? What are the complaints and how could you re-phrase them?

3. How can you show gratitude without comparing?

4. How can you show generosity without causing entitlement?

Trying on the way of Jesus

Choose one of the 7 practices above to try in your family.

4

The Money Manager

The Responsibility of Authority

Ice Breaker

Share a story about something interesting that happened between you and an authority figure.

Lesson

Having authority means being put in charge of something or someone. A person who is given authority is given the job to lead and make decisions in order to care for and protect the things or persons under their authority. And that authority is limited. Every authority will be held responsible for the care they give.[16] Bosses can be fired, policemen can be sent to jail, and Kings can be overthrown.

So, we too, as parents, are limited in the authority we have over a child. It's important to understand the boundaries of the authority we have, or we might use it wrongfully. No one is given full authority over another person's body, emotions, identity, soul, or mind.[17]

---

[16] Hebrews 13:17
[17] Matthew 22:37, Romans 12:1-2

Jesus, who has the greatest authority,[18] shared this story.

> There once was a rich man who was leaving to go on a long trip. Before he left, he called in three of his staff and made them managers of his money while he would be gone. He gave them different amounts, each according to his abilities. To the first one, he gave five thousand dollars; to the second, two thousand dollars; and to the third, one thousand dollars. When the rich man left, the first and second managers went to work right away, making twice as much money. But the man with one thousand dollars dug a hole and buried his in the ground.
>
> After a long time, the rich man came home. He asked the managers what they did with his money. The first manager doubled his money from five thousand to ten thousand. The second manager also doubled his money from two thousand to four thousand. The rich man said to each of them "Good work! You showed me you can be trusted to do well with my money. I'm going to put you in charge of more."
>
> Then the manager who got one thousand dollars came to the rich man and said, "Sir, I knew you expected a lot and I was afraid I might disappoint you, so I hid your money in the ground. Here is the same money you gave me." The rich man said "You are a bad and lazy manager! You know I demand the best! You should have put the money in the bank, where at least I would have gotten a little more money back from interest!"
>
> So the rich man had the one thousand dollars taken away from the bad manager and given to the manager with ten thousand, saying, "Everyone who uses what they have well, will get much more. But

---

[18] Matthew 28:18, John 3:35, Ephesians 1:20-21, Colossians 2:10

those who don't take care of what they have been given, will have it taken away from them."[19]

As parents, we do not own our children. They are God's treasure given into our care for a short period of time. God has made each of us a manager over our own children. Like the servants who managed the rich man's money, we will be held responsible for what we do with them. Our job, as parents, is to take care of our children and help them grow. We are also to protect them, not to serve our own anxieties, but to serve a God who will hold us accountable. Proper care requires taking reasonable risks. If we treat our children like the manager who his money in a hole, they won't grow and mature as God intends them to do. We will be held accountable for poor care, and what authority we have will be taken away.

Questions

1. Who do you think of when you think of a person in authority?

2. How much power should a parent have? How much responsibility?

3. Name some specific responsibilities of being a parent.

4. What are the limits to a parent's authority over a child?

Trying on the way of Jesus

Share what you are going to do this week to take greater responsibility in your parenting

---

[19] Matthew 25:14-29, paraphrased by author for brevity and clarity

5

The Good Shepherd

The Importance of Trust in Obedience

Ice Breaker

Have you ever obeyed someone even though you knew they were wrong? What happened?

Lesson

The Bible tells children to obey and honor their parents.[20] But being obedient does not make a child good, it just makes them easier to manage. If too much focus is put on obedience, a child might start to believe that obedience itself is more important than doing right. But, sometimes doing the right thing means disobeying. Knowing what to do is called discernment, and it's important for children to learn discernment in order to be safe and make good choices. They need to be taught who to obey, who to disobey, and why.

A child taught to obey in response to fear or reward learns to serve his or her own self-interests. Obedience only happens when the child thinks they will be caught. He may look good, but in his heart he is not obedient. Her focus may be on what can be gained for obeying — gifts, praise, and approval — or on protecting her own sense of safety and comfort by

---

[20] Ephesians 6:1-2, Colossians 3:20

17

avoiding the pain of punishment. This kind of obedience creates what Jesus called, "whitewashed tombs,"[21] beautiful on the outside but rotten on the inside.

Jesus, who obeyed perfectly,[22] shared this story.

> The man who does not enter the sheep pen by the door, but climbs in some other way, is a thief and a robber. The one who enters by the door is the shepherd of the sheep. The man who guards the door opens it for him. The sheep listen to the voice of the shepherd. He calls his own sheep, using their names, and leads them out. He brings all of his sheep out, then goes ahead of them and leads them. They follow him because they know his voice. But they will never follow a stranger, but will run away because they don't know his voice.
>
> I am the good shepherd. The good shepherd gives his life for the sheep. The worker who is paid to keep the sheep is different from the shepherd who owns them. The worker sees a wolf coming, runs away, and leaves the sheep alone. Then the wolf attacks the sheep and scatters them. The man runs away because he is only a paid worker and doesn't really care for the sheep. My sheep listen to my voice. I know them, and they follow me.[23]

The sheep have learned to trust the shepherd. They know his voice and his ways. He has named them and knows them individually. They trust him because he doesn't just tell them where to go, he goes ahead of them and leads by example. They know he is good because he defends them from danger and is willing to die for them.[24] The sheep require no stick

---

[21] Matthew 23:27
[22] Philippians 2:8, Romans 5:18, I Peter 1:19, I Peter 2:22
[23] John 10:1-5, 11-13, 27, with some edits for brevity
[24] Matthew 10:16, John 15:13

or reward to get them out of the pen - just the voice of the one they trust.

Children taught to obey for fear or reward will follow anyone who offers either. They become servants of greed and comfort - idols that will betray them. The thief is a false shepherd who will lead them into danger. Even the hired worker, though he may be good, will not protect and love them like the good shepherd. Neither one deserves the loyalty of the sheep.

Children who learn to obey based on love and trust can themselves be trusted. They will obey when no one is watching because they believe that the one who is leading them has their best interests at heart. They will run away from voices that haven't earned their trust, no matter how they pretend or what they offer. God wants children to obey because they love and trust Him.[25] He is the good shepherd and is the most worthy of their obedience and ours.

Questions

1. What is more important, trust or obedience?

2. What's the difference between being obedient and doing what's right or good?

3. How can you teach a child who to obey or disobey?

4. What might the issue be for a child who struggles to obey you?

Trying on the way of Jesus

Discuss with your children who is safe to be trusted and who is not. Explain to them the limits to which they should obey different authorities in their lives, according to the limits of their authority.

---

[25] John 14:15, Romans 6:17

6

The Unlikely Hero

Love and Integrity

Ice Breaker

Share a story of a time when it was really hard to do something good.

Lesson

Integrity is a vital ingredient any healthy relationship. It builds trust and creates closeness. Having integrity means speaking and acting based on who you are and what you believe, regardless of the consequences. It requires being humble, authentic, and bold. A parent with integrity is a blessing to his child.[26] His consistency is a comfort.

As parents, there are times when it is tempting to lie, but if we do, it is a short-lived victory and a decisive betrayal of our integrity. Those who are not truthful about what they really think and feel, who pretend to be better than they are, are hypocrites. Hypocrites hide who they are and what they value most. They pretend to be good so that others will like them. They are overly proud and not worthy of trust. Their children are not fooled for long and learn to lie by their parents' example.

---

[26] Proverbs 20:7

Jesus, known for revealing all truth,[27] shared this story.

> A man was going down the road from Jerusalem to Jericho. Some robbers surrounded him, tore off his clothes, and beat him. Then they left him lying there on the ground almost dead.
>
> It happened that a priest was going down that road. When he saw the wounded man, he did not stop to help him. He walked away. Next, a Levite (a holy man) came near. He saw the hurt man, but he went around him. He would not stop to help him either. He just walked away.
>
> Then a Samaritan man traveled down that road. (Samaritans were hated and considered criminals by the others.) He came to the place where the wounded man was lying. He saw the man and felt very sorry for him. The Samaritan man went to him and poured olive oil and wine on his wounds (to help him). Then he covered the man's wounds with cloth. He put the man on his donkey, and he took him to a hotel. There he cared for the wounded man. The next day, the Samaritan took out two silver coins and gave them to the hotel manager saying, "Take care of this man. If you spend more money on him, I will pay it back to you when I come by again."[28]

The holy men were hypocrites. They only pretended to be holy, but their actions showed that their hearts were not holy. These men who claimed to know God, proved themselves to be liars. God is love. If they knew God, they would know love, and would care for others.[29] The Samaritan didn't pretend to be holy. He didn't hide who he was or that he cared. His actions revealed the kind of person he was.

---

[27] Mark 4:22, John 14:6
[28] Luke 10:30-35, with some edits by the author for clarity
[29] I John 4:7-8

When we have integrity, we act on what we believe, even when we don't feel like it. This doesn't mean we need to be perfect, but humble and honest, especially about our failures.[30] It can be difficult to be humble and vulnerable with those you are in charge of, but an honest parent is easier to trust than a "perfect" parent. Your "yes" means "yes" and your "no" means "no."[31]

Living in such honesty requires great courage. Children need courage to stand up for what's right in the face of pressure to do otherwise. They need courage to be honest about their failures. We can encourage that boldness by giving them confidence that we will offer them grace, help, and prayer in their time of need, just as Jesus has done for us.[32] And like the Samaritan, we can demonstrate our integrity, living what we believe, and showing that we know and love God by loving others sacrificially, even our enemies.[33]

Questions

1. Define integrity in your own words.

2. How might a response to a child who is having a meltdown encourage or discourage them towards authenticity and integrity?

3. When is it most difficult for you to maintain your integrity with your child(ren)?

Trying on the way of Jesus

Choose one area to focus on this week where you can demonstrate more integrity in your relationship with your child(ren).

---

[30] I John 1:8
[31] Matthew 5:37
[32] Hebrews 4:15-16, Ephesians 3:12, James 5:16
[33] Matthew 5:44

7

The Merciful King

Perfecting Love with Mercy

Ice Breaker

Share a story about when you got caught doing something bad, but were shown mercy.

Lesson

To have mercy is to have compassion or forgiveness for someone who should be punished or could be treated harshly.[34] Compassion means caring about someone getting hurt and wanting to stop it. When you are angry, you may want to hurt, blame, shame, and punish the one who hurt you. Maybe they deserve it. But if you have mercy, you don't blame, shame, or punish. Mercy is undeserved forgiveness given at the will of the one, usually in authority, who has been wronged. If it is deserved, it is not mercy.

Mercy does not mean pretending nothing is wrong. Mercy always starts with an uncomfortable truth. Mercy does not allow or condone evil. If we have compassion for those under our care, we point out the wrongdoing, explain why it's wrong, and what it cost.[35] We help them to

---

[34] Matthew 5:3-10
[35] Matthew 18:15

see the consequences without condemnation. The one giving mercy takes the cost upon themselves, not demanding anything of the other person whether payment or payback. As Jesus said, "I desire mercy, not sacrifice."[36]

Love is made perfect by mercy. There is no fear in love. Mercy sets us free from the fear of punishment.[37] It turns anger away from a person and towards the wrongdoing. And the one who is forgiven much loves much in return.[38]

Jesus shared this parable about mercy.

> A king decided to collect the money his servants owed him. One servant owed him thousands of dollars. He was not able to pay the king. So the king ordered that the servant and everything he owned be sold, even his wife and children. The money would be used to pay the king what the servant owed.
>
> But the servant fell on his knees and begged, "Be patient with me. I will pay you everything I owe." The king felt sorry for him. So he told the servant he did not have to pay. He let him go free.
>
> Later, that same servant found another servant who owed him a hundred dollars. He grabbed him around the neck and said, "Pay me the money you owe me!"
>
> The other servant fell on his knees and begged him, "Be patient with me. I will pay you everything I owe." But the first servant refused to be patient. He had the servant put in jail until he could pay everything he owed.

---

[36] Matthew 9:13, Matthew 12:7
[37] I John 4:18, Hebrews 4:16
[38] Luke 7:47

When the other servants saw what happened, they told the king everything that happened. Then the king called his servant in and said, "You evil servant. You begged me to forgive your debt, and I said you did not have to pay anything! So you should have given that other man who serves with you the same mercy I gave you." The master was very angry, so he put the servant in jail to be punished. And he had to stay in jail until he could pay everything he owed.[39]

The first servant was forgiven everything, but did not become merciful like the king. Because we have received mercy, we are called to give mercy. Every wrongdoing provides an opportunity to demonstrate judgment or mercy. Mercy triumphs over judgment.[40]

Having mercy on our children builds them up in love.[41] Control may bring temporary change, but mercy is meant to lead to real change.[42] It reminds our children that our love and acceptance of them are not based on their behavior. We can share in their feelings, having been tempted and having made poor choices ourselves.[43] We all struggle against desires to do evil and know how it feels.[44]

Dietrich Bonheoffer, a pastor who stood up against the Nazis, shared how the experience of mercy from God affected him.

He gave me comfort, forgave all my errors and did not find me guilty of evil. When I was his enemy and did not respect his commandments, he treated me like a friend. When I did him wrong, he returned to me only goodness...I can hardly fathom why

---

[39] Matthew 18:23-34, with some edits by the author
[40] James 2:3
[41] Luke 7:47
[42] Romans 2:4, Romans 12:1-2
[43] Romans 3:23
[44] Ephesians 2:1-4, Romans 7:15-25, Hebrews 4:15

the Lord loves me in this way, why I am so dear to him. I cannot understand how he managed to and wanted to win my heart with his love, all I can say is: "I have received mercy."[45]

Questions

1. How do you feel about mercy? Thankful? Frustrated? Threatened?

2. Do you feel like you've received enough mercy?

3. What are the differences between consequences, judgment, and punishment?

4. When should you not be merciful?

5. What do you think Jesus means by "I desire mercy, not sacrifice"?

Trying on the way of Jesus

Explain mercy to your child. Pick a recurrent bad behavior that your child does and deal with it mercifully (as described in paragraph 2.

---

[45] Bonhoeffer, Dietrich. (2015). La fragilità del male, raccolta di scritti inediti. Retrieved from: http://www.focolare.org/en/news/2015/12/20/ho-ricevuto-misericordia

8

The Forgiving Father

Repentance and Forgiveness

Ice Breaker

Are you quick to say sorry or is it difficult for you? Why?

Lesson

We want our children to be sorry when they do wrong, but words can be empty, sorrow for wrongdoing can be faked, and regret may be only for getting caught. So how can we lead them to true repentance? Repentance means turning away from a way of thinking that leads to sin and turning towards a new way of thinking that leads to good. It's tempting to try to bring about change or remorse by using shame and punishment. But shame is the enemy of true repentance.[46] Shame makes a person stay focused on their wrongdoing. It takes away hope. As shame researcher Brené Brown has said, "Shame corrodes the very part of us that believes we are capable of change."[47]

True repentance does not leave us sad or ashamed, but at peace and full of hope and gratitude. God does not shame or punish us. He does not

---

[46] 2 Corinthians 7:10
[47] Brown, Brené. (2007). I Thought It Was Just Me: Women Reclaiming Power and Courage in a Culture of Shame. Gotham.

ask for tears and promises to do better. His answer to our sin is not that we should avoid Him in shame, try to "fix" things, or "pay the price." He has paid the price, filled with tremendous compassion for us. Even as he hung on the cross he prayed, "Father, forgive them, for they don't know what they are doing."[48] He wants us to be convinced that sin is harmful to us and our relationships, that it drives us away from Him. He calls us to change our ways and to seek after Him. "We don't repent in hopes that we might be loved, embraced, and forgiven, but because we are embraced, we repent."[49]

Jesus shared this story about a repentant son and a forgiving father.

> There was a man who had two sons. The younger son said to his father, "Give me everything of yours now that I would get when you're dead." So the father divided his wealth between his two sons.

> A few days later the younger son packed up all his stuff and left. He traveled far away to another country, and wasted his money living like a fool. After he spent everything he had, there was a terrible famine throughout the country. He was hungry and needed money. So he got a job feeding pigs. He was so hungry that he wanted to eat the pig's food, but no one gave him anything.

> The son realized that he had been very foolish. He thought, "All my father's hired workers have plenty of food. But here I am, almost dead because I have nothing to eat. I will go to my father and say, 'Father, I have sinned against God and have done wrong to you. I am no longer worthy to be called your son. But let me be like one of your hired workers.'" So he headed back to his Father.

> While the son was still a long way off, his father saw him coming.

---

[48] Luke 23:34
[49] PCC LOL Curriculum (2015), Romans 2:4

So he ran to him and hugged and kissed him. The son said, "Father, I have sinned against God and have done wrong to you. I am no longer worthy to be called your son."

But the father said to his servants, "Hurry! Bring the best clothes and put them on him. Put a ring on his finger and sandals on his feet. Kill our best calf so that we can celebrate with plenty to eat. My son was dead, but now he is alive again! He was lost, but now he is found!" So they began to have a party.

The older son was heading into the house from working in the field when heard the sound of music and dancing. He asked a servant boy, "What's all this about?" The boy said, "Your brother has come back, and your father killed the best calf to eat. He is happy because he has his son back safe and sound."

The older son got angry and would not go to the party. So his father went out and begged him to come in. But he said to his father, "For all these years I have worked like a slave for you. I have always done what you told me to do, and you never gave me even a young goat for a party with my friends. But then this son of yours comes home after wasting your money on prostitutes, and you kill the best calf for him!"

The father said, "My son, you are always with me, and everything I have is yours. But this was a day to be happy and celebrate. Your brother was dead, but now he is alive. He was lost, but now he is found."[50]

Even though the younger son had rudely demanded and wasted his father's money only to return home in a dirty and shameful state, the father responded with joy at his return. He did not hesitate to throw his

---

[50] Luke 15:11-32

arms around his child, did not shame him, nor demand repayment. He was full of love and mercy towards his child, and more concerned with his restoration than his wrongdoing. Neither did he shame the older son who was being self-righteous and judgmental. He too, was sought after and invited to the party.

Children may need help to acknowledge their sin and sinfulness. This doesn't mean telling children they are bad, have lost their worth, or are repulsive to God. Maybe it means letting them experience the consequences of their choices, like the father allowed the younger son to do. Maybe it means speaking truth with gentleness, like how the father spoke to the older son. Correcting with kindness, mercy, and gentleness can be a powerful motivator for change.[51] It tells our children that we value our relationship with them over their behavior. It gives them confidence that our love is not dependent on their being good. It encourages them to come to us when they do wrong, because they know we will respond with compassion, help, and prayer.[52]

True repentance produces gratitude for mercy, a refreshed heart, joy at being accepted, and love. It gives hope and empowers change. No blame, no shame, no promises.

Questions

1. What's the difference between repentance and feeling sorry?

2. What are the barriers to true repentance? How can we inadvertently direct our children away from true repentance?

3. How can you tell if your child has truly repented?

---

[51] 2 Timothy 2:24-25
[52] Matthew 15:22, 17:15, Mark 9:14-29, Luke 23:34, Romans 8:34, James 5:16

4. What can you do to foster true repentance if you believe that your child hasn't truly repented?

Trying on the way of Jesus

When your child does wrong this week, emphasize the love and mercy you and God have for your child more than the wrongdoing. Pray over your child as Jesus prayed, "Father, forgive them, for they don't know what they are doing."

9

The Persistent Neighbor

The Value of Never Giving Up

Ice Breaker

Share a time when you fought long and hard for something. What kept you going?

Lesson

It has been said that the greatest indicator of success is not intelligence, talent, or fortune, but persistence.[53] Persistence is responding to adversity by holding firm or pushing on towards a goal, overcoming any barriers and obstacles. It means not quitting, even when it's difficult. Persistence builds discipline[54] and produces hope.[55] It is the path to maturity.[56]

Some children seem to be naturally more persistent than others even early in their youth. They don't easily give up on new tasks. However, this great natural quality has yet to be fully paired with their still developing minds, and they lack the ability to reason and the knowledge required to make good decisions about what's worth fighting for. Some words that may be

---

[53] Proverbs 10:4
[54] Hebrews 12:7
[55] Romans 5:3-4
[56] James 1:4

used to describe a persistent person are: stubborn, persevering, enduring, determined, committed, diligent, or having "grit."

Other children are quicker to give up. They are more skilled at surrender. They are quicker to submit to authority, and can be "easier" children to manage. However, they are at risk of becoming people-pleasers who will give in to pressure from anyone, including bad influences. They often lack the persistence needed to accomplish difficult tasks and to stand up to peer pressure.

Jesus, who persevered to the point of death,[57] shared the following parable about persistence.

> Suppose one of you has a friend and goes to him at midnight and says to him, "Friend, lend me three loaves of bread, because a friend of mine on a journey has come to me, and I don't have anything to offer him." Then he will answer from inside and say, "Don't bother me! The door is already locked, and my children and I have gone to bed. I can't get up to give you anything." I tell you, even though he won't get up and give him anything because he is his friend, yet because of his friend's persistence, he will get up and give him as much as he needs.[58]

Being focused or single-minded is the foundation of perseverance. The man doesn't give up knocking and asking because he is focused on getting the bread for his guests, not on what's in his way. He's not letting the time of day or the fact that his neighbor is sleeping stop him. He doesn't see his "no," as final, but temporary.

It's easier to persevere if we focus on our goals and the actions that will help us achieve our goals. Jesus endured suffering and death[59] by focusing

---

[57] Hebrews 12:2
[58] Luke 11:5-8
[59] Hebrews 12:2

on the joy that would come after. At any moment through being beaten and dying he could've walked away, but he persisted. He endured. What looked like failure was actually the path to success and victory. It is through focusing on Jesus that we can find the strength to persevere.[60]

Children need help to know when to persist and when to surrender. They need to have a strong sense of what they are aiming for and why. This will motivate them to keep going when they want to quit. They also need us to model persistence. They will feel more secure with a parent who will not give up on them, who will hold the boundaries, and who will fight for them. They need to be reminded that they aren't defined by failure, but by God — and God does not give up on us.[61] They need us to help them rebound from failure, to point out the value of their efforts, and to help them discover what they can learn from failure. They need to be reminded of the hope we have in Jesus. Encourage them that they will see good results if they hope in the gospel and keep doing good.[62] As Jesus said, "Ask and it will be given to you; seek, and you will find; knock, and it will be opened to you. For everyone who asks, receives; and he who seeks, finds; and to him who knocks, it will be opened."

Questions

1. What does it mean to be persistent?

2. What are some things you should not persist in that you sometimes do?

3. What are some things you should persist in that are worth lots of effort?

---

[60] Colossians 1:11, Philippians 4:13
[61] Philippians 1:6
[62] Galatians 6:9, Colossians 1:22-23, Philippians 1:27-28

Trying on the way of Jesus

Encourage your children towards persistence this week. Don't do for them what they can do for themselves. Whether or not they succeed, praise their effort and endurance.

10

The Rich Fool

Finding Contentment

Ice Breaker

If you received a million-dollar gift today, what would you do with it?

Lesson

Parents are providers. We are responsible for making sure our children have food, clothing, a place to live, proper health care, and more. Of course, we like to provide much more than just what is needed. We give children things like toys, treats, and fun experiences. Often we give up something for ourselves for the joy of giving to our children.

As children grow older, they gradually take on more responsibility to provide for themselves. They learn to cook, wash their clothes, and make their beds. Eventually, they start to work and pay for the things they want and need.

Jesus, who trusted the Father for all his needs,[63] shared this story about a rich young man.

> There was a rich man who had some land. His land grew a very
> good crop of food. He thought to himself, "What will I do? I have

---

[63] John 14:31, Matthew 26:39, Matthew 4:4, Luke 5:16

no place to keep all my crops." Then he said, "I know what I will do. I will tear down my barns and build bigger barns! I will put all my wheat and good things together in my new barns. Then I can say to myself, I have many good things stored. I have saved enough for many years. Rest, eat, drink, and enjoy life!"

But God said to that man, "Foolish man! Tonight you will die. So what about the things you prepared for yourself? Who will get those things now?"[64]

This rich young man had so much that it had become a problem. What should he do with all these extra crops? If he had been grateful and recognized all that he had been given was a generous gift, in fact, he might have made a different choice. He might have said, "I know what I will do. As I have received I will give. I will give generously to all who are hungry and in need."[65] But his actions showed he was consumed with himself.[66] He did not see the needs of those around him. He did not trust in God to provide for the future, even though He had already abundantly provided. The man could have turned those earthly riches into eternal riches by giving them away.

Our culture feeds into the feeling that we don't have enough. "If your closet is full, you need a bigger closet." Advertisements create discontentment and promise that acquiring things will solve it. But this is a lie. You have access to the infinite riches of God, and He is willing and able to meet your needs. You never have reason to worry.[67] God knows what we need and will provide.[68] Perhaps, just as too much food can make us sick to our stomachs, too many earthly possessions can make us sick

---

[64] Luke 12:16-20
[65] Mark 10:21, I Timothy 6:6-10
[66] Philippians 4:19, Hebrews 13:5
[67] Luke 12:27-34
[68] Philippians 4:19, Hebrews 13:5

to our souls. Just as each person needs a different amount of food, perhaps each of our souls has a different need on this earth.

When we give generously to our children and others, we reflect the generosity of our heavenly Father. We can let go of earthly possessions easily when we more greatly value heavenly riches. The things of earth will not last forever, but the things we do for God's kingdom will be our treasures in eternity.[69]

Questions

1. Do you feel like you have enough? If not, what would be enough?

2. What are some things you tend to hoard? Why?

3. How can you help your children to be convinced they have enough?

Trying on the way of Jesus

Choose something you have too much of and give it to someone in need. Talk through it with your child, demonstrating a spirit of gratitude, contentment, and generosity.

---

[69] 2 Corinthians 9:8

EPILOGUE

Christ's life provides many more examples for us as parents. Isaiah called Jesus the "Everlasting Father" (Isaiah 9:6). He was fatherly towards his followers and referred to his disciples as "little children" (Matthew 11:25, Mark 10:24, John 13:33). He acted like a father: initiating, providing, protecting, guiding, correcting, teaching, preparing, modeling, encouraging, and loving those entrusted to his care. He said, "I will not leave you as orphans" (John 14:18). He has left his Spirit and his word with us. "Every Scripture is God-breathed and profitable for teaching, for reproof, for correction, and for instruction in righteousness, that the man of God may be complete, thoroughly equipped for every good work," including parenting (2 Timothy 3:16-17).

If you don't yet have a personal connection with Jesus, you've gotten to know some of the character and person of Christ through these lessons. He is the gardener who plants the truth in your heart, the humble begotten Son of God who took the form of man to serve and save us, washing our dirty feet and dying for our sins. He is generous and the grateful. He is responsible with his authority and perfectly obedient. He is the unlikely hero, full of love, mercy, and integrity. He is forgiving, persistent, and generous.

God desires good things for you and to be with you as a Father. But, to be close with God, who is holy and perfect, you must first be purified. Because of His grace, His desire for your good, this purification has been made available to all who trust in the perfect life and merciful sacrifice of His Son, Jesus. Your every crime is paid for by his death. Your imperfections are covered by his perfect life. By connecting with Christ, your hang ups and old habits lose hold of you, and you enter into a new life connected to the risen Jesus. His Spirit will guide you into the good life of "love, joy, peace, patience, kindness, goodness, faith, gentleness, self-control" that God has always intended for you (Galatians 5:22-23, Ephesians 2:10), the life empowered to parent in Christ.

FOR FURTHER STUDY

If you are interested in further exploring what it means to parent in Christ, you can read the first book in this series,
"Parenting in Christ: Treasures for Parenting from Jesus."
Topics include humility, gratitude, authority, obedience, integrity, mission, repentance, gentleness, righteousness, and parenting in the Spirit.

Parenting in Christ lays a biblical foundation for how to parent your children in grace and truth. It challenges you to first look within yourself and your relationship with Christ, and then look outward to your raising your children as disciples of Christ.
- Marie

Parenting In Christ eased my anxiety as a parent, silenced my self-criticism and helped me to focus on the way of Jesus with my children.
- Sarah

This book inspired me to learn to apply the fruits of the Spirit to share (and model) the love of Christ with my children. It was grounded in Scripture, and there was also so much real world advice that was incredibly helpful to me.
- Nellie

It's so refreshing to see guidance to parenthood that starts with the heart of Jesus, versus a list of do's and don'ts. This study is full of scripture and is intended to point us all (parents and our children) to the heart of Jesus.
- Carol

Made in United States
North Haven, CT
21 August 2023

40581573R00039